MOTAB

Transforming lives, one behavior at a time- that's the power of MOTAB

Chapter I: Introduction to MOTAB

A. Purpose and scope of the MOTAB guidebook

The Management of Techniques and Behaviors (MOTAB) guidebook is designed to provide a comprehensive framework for using Applied Behavior Analysis (ABA) principles to support adult individuals with intellectual and developmental disabilities (ID/DD) who are also considered high-risk forensic adults. This guidebook aims to equip professionals, caregivers, and support staff with evidence-based strategies and tools to effectively address the complex needs of this population, promote positive behavior change, and enhance their quality of life.

The MOTAB guidebook is intended to be a practical resource that bridges the gap between research and practice, offering step-by-step guidance on how to assess, plan, implement, and evaluate ABA interventions in the context of adult ID/DD high-risk forensic populations. It covers a wide range of topics, from understanding the unique challenges faced by this population to developing individualized support plans, implementing behavioral interventions, and promoting community integration.

The guidebook is designed for use by a variety of professionals, including behavior analysts, psychologists, social workers, case managers, and direct support staff who work with adult ID/DD high-risk forensic individuals across various settings, such as community-based programs, residential facilities, and forensic treatment centers. It emphasizes the importance of a collaborative, multidisciplinary approach to support this population, recognizing that successful outcomes require the coordination and integration of multiple services and systems.

In the guidebook, readers will find practical tools, case studies, and real-world examples that illustrate how to apply ABA principles in the context of adult ID/DD high-risk forensic populations. The ultimate goal of the MOTAB guidebook is to empower professionals and caregivers with the knowledge and skills needed to effectively support this population, reduce the risk of criminal recidivism, and promote their successful integration into the community.

The MOTAB guidebook also addresses the importance of cultural competence and diversity in working with adult ID/DD high-risk forensic individuals. It recognizes that this population is diverse in terms of race, ethnicity, language, socioeconomic status, and other cultural factors and that these factors can influence their experiences, needs, and responses to intervention. The guidebook provides strategies for adapting ABA interventions to be culturally responsive and inclusive, and for addressing potential biases and disparities in the delivery of services.

In addition, the MOTAB guidebook emphasizes the importance of a strengths-based approach that focuses on the individual's abilities, interests, and aspirations, rather than solely on their deficits or risk factors. It provides strategies for identifying and building upon the individual's strengths and resources, and for promoting their active participation and self-determination in the treatment process.

The guidebook also addresses the importance of family and caregiver involvement in supporting adult ID/DD high-risk forensic individuals. It recognizes that families and caregivers play a critical role in promoting positive outcomes and reducing the risk of recidivism, and provides strategies for engaging and empowering them as active partners in the treatment process.

Finally, the MOTAB guidebook emphasizes the importance of ongoing monitoring, evaluation, and quality improvement in the delivery of ABA interventions for adult ID/DD high-risk forensic individuals. It provides strategies for collecting and analyzing data on treatment outcomes, identifying areas for improvement, and making data-driven decisions to optimize the effectiveness and efficiency of interventions over time.

B. Overview of ABA and its relevance to supporting adult ID/DD high-risk forensic individuals

Applied Behavior Analysis (ABA) is a scientific approach to understanding and changing behavior based on the principles of learning and motivation. ABA focuses on identifying the environmental factors that influence behavior and developing individualized strategies to promote positive outcomes. Some of the core principles of ABA include:

1. **Reinforcement**: Increasing the likelihood of a behavior occurring in the future by providing positive consequences following the behavior.

2. **Punishment**: Decreasing the likelihood of a behavior occurring in the future by providing negative consequences following the behavior.

3. **Extinction:** Reducing the frequency of a behavior by withholding the reinforcement that previously maintained the behavior. Beware, as this may escalate the behaviors before reducing them.

4. **Stimulus control**: Establishing the presence of certain environmental cues that signal the availability of reinforcement for a particular behavior.

ABA has been widely recognized as an effective intervention for individuals with ID/DD, as it provides a structured, data-driven approach to addressing challenging behaviors and teaching adaptive skills. In the context of adult ID/DD high-risk forensic individuals, ABA can be particularly valuable in:

1. Assessing the functions of challenging behaviors:

By conducting functional behavior assessments (FBAs), professionals can identify the environmental factors that trigger and maintain challenging behaviors, such as aggression, self-injury, or sexual offending.

2. Developing individualized behavior support plans:

Based on the results of the FBA, professionals can develop targeted interventions that address the specific needs and risk factors of each individual, using evidence-based strategies such as positive reinforcement, functional communication training, and teaching replacement behaviors.

3. Teaching adaptive skills:

ABA can be used to teach a wide range of adaptive skills, such as daily living skills, social skills, and vocational skills, which can enhance individuals' independence and reduce their risk of criminal recidivism.

4. Promoting generalization and maintenance:

ABA emphasizes the importance of programming for generalization and maintenance, ensuring that the skills and behaviors learned in treatment settings transfer to real-world contexts and are sustained over time.

By applying ABA principles, professionals can develop comprehensive, individualized support plans that address the complex needs of adult ID/DD high-risk forensic individuals, promoting their successful integration into the community and reducing the risk of criminal recidivism.

ABA also emphasizes the importance of data collection and analysis in monitoring treatment progress and making data-driven decisions. By regularly collecting and analyzing data on target behaviors, professionals can identify patterns and trends, evaluate the effectiveness of interventions, and make timely adjustments to optimize outcomes.

In addition, ABA recognizes the importance of a team-based approach to treatment, involving collaboration and coordination among multiple professionals and stakeholders, such as behavior analysts, psychologists, social workers, probation officers, and community providers. This team-based approach ensures that interventions are comprehensive, consistent, and well-coordinated across settings and systems.

ABA also emphasizes the importance of training and support for caregivers and staff who work with adult ID/DD high-risk forensic individuals. By providing ongoing training and coaching in ABA principles and strategies, professionals can ensure that interventions are implemented with fidelity and that caregivers and staff are equipped to effectively support individuals in their daily lives.

Finally, ABA recognizes the importance of considering the broader social, cultural, and political context in which adult ID/DD high-risk forensic individuals live and receive services. It emphasizes the need for advocacy and systems change efforts to address barriers to access and equity in services and to promote policies and practices that support the full inclusion and participation of this population in their communities.

C. Unique challenges faced by this population

Adult individuals with ID/DD who are also high-risk forensic adults face a complex set of challenges that require specialized support and intervention. These challenges may include:

1. Comorbid mental health conditions: Many individuals with ID/DD also experience co-occurring mental health disorders, such as depression, anxiety, or personality disorders, which can further complicate their behavioral presentation and treatment needs. These comorbid conditions may interact with their ID/DD and forensic risk factors, creating a complex clinical picture that requires a comprehensive, integrated approach to assessment and treatment.

2. Limited adaptive skills: Individuals with ID/DD may struggle with daily living skills, communication, and social interactions, which can increase their vulnerability and risk of involvement with the criminal justice system. These limitations in adaptive skills may make it more difficult for them to navigate complex social situations, understand the consequences of their actions, and advocate for their needs, increasing their risk of exploitation or victimization.

3. **Stigma and discrimination**: This population often faces significant stigma and discrimination, both due to their disability and their forensic involvement, which can create barriers to accessing appropriate support and services. They may be viewed as "challenging" or "difficult to serve," leading to a lack of appropriate community-based resources and a higher risk of institutionalization or incarceration.

4. **Complexity of the criminal justice system**: Navigating the criminal justice system can be particularly challenging for individuals with ID/DD, who may have difficulty understanding legal processes, communicating with legal professionals, and advocating for their rights. They may be more vulnerable to coercion or false confessions, and may not receive appropriate accommodations or support throughout the legal process.

5. Limited community resources: There is often a shortage of specialized community-based services and supports tailored to the needs of adult ID/DD high-risk forensic individuals, which can hinder their successful reintegration and increase the risk of recidivism. These individuals may require a range of services, including mental health treatment, substance abuse treatment, vocational training, and housing support, which may not be readily available or accessible in many communities.

6. Challenges in family and social support systems: Adult ID/DD high-risk forensic individuals may have limited or strained relationships with family members and social support systems, which can further exacerbate their risk factors and hinder their ability to access necessary resources and services. They may have experienced abuse, neglect, or exploitation within their family or social networks, leading to a lack of trust and difficulty forming healthy relationships.

7. Difficulty with self-advocacy and self-determination: Due to their cognitive and communication challenges, adult ID/DD high-risk forensic individuals may struggle with self-advocacy and self-determination, which can limit their ability to make informed choices about their treatment, services, and life goals.

This can lead to a lack of engagement in treatment and a higher risk of non-compliance with legal requirements or community supervision.

8. Historical trauma and adverse life experiences: Many adult ID/DD high-risk forensic individuals have experienced significant trauma and adverse life experiences, such as abuse, neglect, or institutionalization, which can contribute to the development of challenging behaviors and mental health conditions. These experiences may also create barriers to trust and engagement in treatment, requiring a trauma-informed approach to support and intervention.

9. Lack of research and evidence-based practices: Despite the significant needs and challenges faced by adult ID/DD high-risk forensic individuals, there is a limited body of research and evidence-based practices specifically tailored to this population. Many interventions and supports have been developed and validated for individuals with ID/DD or for forensic populations separately, but there is a need for more research and development of integrated interventions that address the unique needs of this population.

10. Inadequate training and expertise among professionals: Many professionals who work with adult ID/DD high-risk forensic individuals, such as mental health providers, probation officers, and direct support staff, may lack specialized training and expertise in working with this population. This can lead to a lack of understanding of their unique needs and challenges, and the use of inappropriate or ineffective interventions.

11. Systemic barriers and fragmentation of services: Adult ID/DD high-risk forensic individuals often interact with multiple systems and services, such as the criminal justice system, mental health system, and developmental disabilities system, which may operate in silos and have different eligibility criteria, funding streams, and service models. This fragmentation of services can create barriers to access and coordination of care, leading to gaps in services and poor outcomes.

12. Ethical and legal considerations: Supporting adult ID/DD high-risk forensic individuals raises a range of ethical and legal considerations, such as balancing individual rights and autonomy with public safety, obtaining informed consent for treatment and research, and ensuring due process in legal proceedings.

Professionals working with this population must navigate these complex ethical and legal issues while also providing effective and compassionate care.

13. Risk of recidivism and community safety concerns: Adult ID/DD high-risk forensic individuals may have a history of criminal behavior or present with risk factors for future offending, such as impulsivity, aggression, or sexual behavior problems. Supporting this population requires a delicate balance of promoting individual rehabilitation and community reintegration while also ensuring public safety and managing risk.

14. Intersectionality and diversity considerations: Adult ID/DD high-risk forensic individuals come from diverse backgrounds and may face multiple forms of marginalization and oppression based on their race, ethnicity, gender, sexual orientation, socioeconomic status, and other factors. Supporting this population requires an intersectional approach that recognizes and addresses the unique challenges and barriers faced by individuals with multiple marginalized identities.

15. Lack of funding and resources: Providing comprehensive and effective support and services for adult ID/DD high-risk forensic individuals requires significant funding and resources, which may be limited or unavailable in many communities. This lack of funding and resources can create barriers to access and quality of care and may perpetuate the cycle of marginalization and criminalization experienced by this population.

16. Stigma and misconceptions among the general public: Adult ID/DD high-risk forensic individuals often face significant stigma and misconceptions among the general public, who may view them as dangerous, unpredictable, or beyond rehabilitation. These negative attitudes and beliefs can create barriers to community acceptance and integration and may perpetuate the cycle of marginalization and criminalization experienced by this population.

By acknowledging and addressing these unique challenges, the MOTAB guidebook aims to provide a comprehensive framework for supporting this population and promoting positive outcomes. It emphasizes the importance of a person-centered, strengths-based approach that considers the individual's unique needs, preferences, and goals, while also addressing their forensic risk factors and promoting community safety. The guidebook provides strategies for collaborating with multidisciplinary teams, advocating for appropriate services and supports, and empowering individuals to achieve their full potential as valued members of their

communities.

Chapter II. Understanding ID/DD and Forensic Risk Factors

A. Defining intellectual and developmental disabilities

Intellectual and developmental disabilities (ID/DD) are a group of conditions

characterized by significant limitations in both intellectual functioning and

adaptive behavior, which cover many everyday social and practical skills. These

disabilities originate before the age of 18 and can impact an individual's ability to

learn, reason, problem-solve, and navigate social situations.

Intellectual disabilities are characterized by an IQ score of 70 or below and can

range from mild to profound in severity. Individuals with mild ID may have

difficulty with abstract thinking, planning, and problem-solving, but may be able to

live independently with some support. Those with more severe forms of ID may

require more extensive support and may have significant limitations in

communication, self-care, and decision-making.

Developmental disabilities are a broader category that includes intellectual disabilities, as well as other conditions that impact an individual's physical, cognitive, or behavioral development. Examples of developmental disabilities include autism spectrum disorder, cerebral palsy, and fetal alcohol spectrum disorders. These conditions can co-occur with intellectual disabilities and can present additional challenges and support needs.

It is important to recognize that individuals with ID/DD are a heterogeneous group, with a wide range of strengths, challenges, and support needs. While they may have limitations in certain areas, they also have unique talents, interests, and abilities that should be recognized and nurtured. Supporting individuals with ID/DD requires an individualized, person-centered approach that focuses on their strengths and goals, rather than solely on their deficits or limitations.

The definition and diagnosis of ID/DD have evolved, and continue to be shaped by advances in research, policy, and advocacy. In recent years, there has been a shift towards a more social and ecological understanding of disability, which recognizes that an individual's functioning is not solely determined by their impairments, but also by the social, cultural, and environmental factors that shape their experiences and opportunities.

This shift has led to a greater emphasis on promoting inclusion, self-determination, and community participation for individuals with ID/DD, and on addressing the systemic barriers and inequities that limit their full participation in society. Supporting individuals with ID/DD requires not only providing individualized interventions and support but also working to create more inclusive and accessible communities that value and embrace diversity.

B. Comorbidity of ID/DD and forensic risk factors

Individuals with ID/DD are at increased risk for involvement with the criminal justice system, both as victims and as offenders. Research has consistently shown that individuals with ID/DD are overrepresented in the criminal justice system and that they face unique challenges and vulnerabilities at all stages of the legal process.

Several factors contribute to the increased risk of criminal justice involvement among individuals with ID/DD. These include:

1. **Cognitive and social vulnerabilities**: Individuals with ID/DD may have difficulty understanding and navigating complex social situations, and may be more vulnerable to manipulation, coercion, or exploitation by others. They may also have difficulty understanding the consequences of their actions and may engage in impulsive or risky behavior without fully understanding the potential risks or legal consequences.

2. **Comorbid mental health conditions**: Many individuals with ID/DD also have co-occurring mental health conditions, such as depression, anxiety, or personality disorders, which can further increase their risk of criminal behavior or victimization. These conditions may interact with their cognitive and social vulnerabilities, creating a complex set of risk factors that require specialized assessment and intervention.

3. **Trauma and adverse life experiences**: Individuals with ID/DD are at increased risk for experiencing trauma and adverse life experiences, such as abuse, neglect, or bullying, which can contribute to the development of behavioral and mental health problems. These experiences may also create a sense of learned

helplessness or distrust of authority figures, which can make it more difficult for individuals to seek help or report victimization.

4. Lack of access to appropriate services and supports: Many individuals with ID/DD do not receive the specialized services and support they need to address their cognitive, social, and mental health needs. This lack of access can exacerbate their vulnerabilities and increase their risk of criminal justice involvement, as they may engage in behaviors that are seen as disruptive or threatening in the absence of appropriate support.

5. Criminogenic risk factors: Like any other population, individuals with ID/DD may also be exposed to criminogenic risk factors, such as substance abuse, antisocial peers, or criminal thinking patterns, which can increase their likelihood of engaging in criminal behavior. However, these risk factors may interact with their ID/DD in unique ways, requiring specialized assessment and intervention approaches.

It is important to recognize that the relationship between ID/DD and criminal justice involvement is complex and multifaceted, and cannot be reduced to a simple causal link. While individuals with ID/DD may be at increased risk for criminal behavior or victimization, *the vast majority of individuals with these conditions do not engage in criminal activity, and should not be stigmatized or presumed to be dangerous based solely on their diagnosis.*

Supporting individuals with ID/DD who are involved in the criminal justice system requires a collaborative, multidisciplinary approach that addresses their cognitive, social, and mental health needs, while also promoting accountability and community safety. This may involve specialized assessment tools, such as the ID/DD-specific risk assessment instruments, as well as adapted interventions that are tailored to the unique learning styles and support needs of this population.

It is also important to recognize the systemic factors that contribute to the overrepresentation of individuals with ID/DD in the criminal justice system, such as the lack of community-based services and supports, the criminalization of mental illness and disability, and the inadequate training of law enforcement and legal professionals in working with this population. Addressing these systemic issues requires a broader, more proactive approach that focuses on prevention, early intervention, and community-based support, rather than relying solely on the criminal justice system to manage the needs of this vulnerable population.

C. Impact of ID/DD on behavior and decision-making

Individuals with ID/DD may exhibit a range of behavioral and decision-making challenges that can impact their functioning and increase their risk of criminal justice involvement. These challenges may be related to their cognitive limitations, social skills deficits, or comorbid mental health conditions, and may require specialized assessment and intervention approaches.

One common behavioral challenge among individuals with ID/DD is aggression, which may be verbal, physical, or sexual. Aggression may be related to a variety of factors, such as frustration, sensory overload, difficulty communicating needs or desires, etc. Individuals with ID/DD may also have difficulty with impulse control and emotional regulation, which can lead to impulsive or reactive aggression in response to perceived threats or stressors.

Another behavioral challenge that may be more common among individuals with ID/DD is self-injurious behavior, which involves intentional self-harm such as head-banging, biting, or scratching. Self-injurious behavior may serve a variety of functions, such as sensory stimulation, attention-seeking, or escape from demands, and may require a comprehensive functional assessment to identify the underlying causes and develop appropriate interventions.

Individuals with ID/DD may also exhibit socially inappropriate or offensive behaviors, such as public masturbation, unwanted touching, or invasion of personal space. These behaviors may be related to a lack of social skills or understanding of social norms and may require explicit instruction and behavioral interventions to promote more appropriate social interactions.

In terms of decision-making, individuals with ID/DD may have difficulty with abstract reasoning, planning, and problem-solving, which can impact their ability to make informed and responsible choices. They may be more susceptible to peer pressure or manipulation by others and may have difficulty weighing the short-term and long-term consequences of their actions.

Individuals with ID/DD may also have limited knowledge or understanding of legal concepts such as guilt, innocence, and plea bargaining, which can impact their ability to participate in their defense and make informed decisions about their case. They may be more likely to confess to crimes they did not commit, or to agree to plea bargains without fully understanding the implications.

Supporting individuals with ID/DD who exhibit behavioral or decision-making challenges requires a comprehensive, individualized approach that addresses their unique needs and strengths. This may involve functional behavior assessments to identify the underlying causes of challenging behaviors, as well as positive behavior support plans that focus on teaching replacement behaviors and skills.

It may also involve decision-making supports, such as visual aids, simplified language, or additional time for processing information, to help individuals with ID/DD make informed and responsible choices. Legal professionals working with individuals with ID/DD may need to adapt their communication style and provide accommodations to ensure that these individuals can meaningfully participate in the legal process.

In addition to individual-level interventions, supporting individuals with ID/DD who exhibit behavioral or decision-making challenges also requires a systemic approach that addresses the broader social and environmental factors that contribute to these challenges. This may involve advocating for increased funding and access to community-based services and supports, as well as promoting greater awareness and understanding of ID/DD among legal and criminal justice professionals.

It is important to recognize that individuals with ID/DD are a diverse and heterogeneous group and that their behavioral and decision-making challenges are not inherent to their diagnosis, but are often a product of the complex interplay between individual, social, and environmental factors. By taking a holistic and individualized approach that focuses on strengths, skills, and supports, we can promote greater self-determination, community inclusion, and quality of life for individuals with ID/DD who are involved in the criminal justice system.

Chapter III. Principles of ABA in the Context of ID/DD and Forensic Populations

A. Adapting ABA principles to meet the needs of adult ID/DD high-risk forensic individuals

Applied Behavior Analysis (ABA) is a scientific approach to understanding and changing behavior that has been widely used in the fields of education, healthcare, and human services. While ABA has traditionally been associated with the treatment of individuals with autism spectrum disorder (ASD), its principles and techniques can be effectively adapted to meet the needs of adult individuals with intellectual and developmental disabilities (ID/DD) who are also involved in the criminal justice system.

One of the key principles of ABA is the focus on observable and measurable behaviors, rather than on internal states or traits. This emphasis on objective data collection and analysis is particularly relevant in working with adult ID/DD high-risk forensic individuals, as it allows for the identification of specific behaviors that may be contributing to criminal justice involvement, as well as the development of targeted interventions to address those behaviors.

Another key principle of ABA is the use of positive reinforcement to increase desired behaviors and decrease challenging behaviors. In working with adult ID/DD high-risk forensic individuals, it is important to identify individualized reinforcers that are meaningful and motivating to the individual and to use those reinforcers consistently and strategically to shape behavior over time. This may involve collaborating with the individual and their support network to identify preferences and interests and incorporating those into the intervention plan.

ABA also emphasizes the importance of functional assessment, which involves identifying the underlying causes or functions of behavior, rather than simply focusing on the topography or form of the behavior. In working with adult ID/DD high-risk forensic individuals, functional assessment may involve gathering information from multiple sources, such as interviews with the individual and their support network, direct observation of behavior in different settings, and review of relevant records and documents. This comprehensive approach can help to identify patterns of behavior and environmental factors that may be contributing to criminal justice involvement and to develop interventions that address those factors.

Adapting ABA principles to meet the needs of adult ID/DD high-risk forensic individuals also requires a recognition of the unique challenges and complexities of this population. For example, individuals with ID/DD may have cognitive limitations that impact their ability to understand and respond to traditional behavioral interventions and may require modifications such as visual supports, simplified language, or additional prompting and reinforcement. Similarly, individuals with a history of trauma or adverse life experiences may require a trauma-sensitive approach that prioritizes safety, trust, and collaboration.

Another important consideration in adapting ABA principles to this population is the need for cultural competence and responsiveness. Adult ID/DD high-risk forensic individuals may come from diverse cultural and linguistic backgrounds and may have different values, beliefs, and communication styles that impact their engagement with behavioral interventions. It is important for practitioners to be aware of these differences and to adapt their approach accordingly, such as by using culturally relevant examples and reinforcers, or by involving family members or other cultural brokers in the intervention process.

Finally, adapting ABA principles to meet the needs of adult ID/DD high-risk forensic individuals requires a recognition of the broader systemic and societal factors that contribute to their involvement in the criminal justice system. This may include advocating for increased access to community-based services and supports, addressing issues of poverty, discrimination, and marginalization, and promoting greater awareness and understanding of ID/DD among criminal justice professionals. By taking a holistic and systemic approach, practitioners can help to create more inclusive and equitable communities that support the full participation and inclusion of individuals with ID/DD.

B. Importance of person-centered planning and support

Person-centered planning and support is a key component of effective behavioral intervention for adult ID/DD high-risk forensic individuals. This approach prioritizes the individual's unique strengths, needs, and preferences, and involves them and their support network as active participants in the planning and implementation of services.

One of the core principles of person-centered planning is the recognition that individuals with ID/DD are experts in their own lives, and have the right to make choices and decisions about their care and support. This means that behavioral interventions should be developed in collaboration with the individual and their support network, rather than being imposed upon them by professionals or external authorities.

Person-centered planning also emphasizes the importance of focusing on the individual's strengths and capabilities, rather than solely on their deficits or challenges. This may involve identifying and building upon the individual's interests, talents, and accomplishments, and using those as a foundation for developing goals and interventions. By focusing on strengths and positive attributes, practitioners can help promote a sense of self-efficacy and empowerment and create opportunities for success and growth.

Another key aspect of person-centered planning is the recognition that individuals with ID/DD are part of a broader social and community context and that their needs and goals are shaped by the relationships and environments in which they live. This means that behavioral interventions should be developed in collaboration with the individual's support network, including family members, friends, and community partners, and should be integrated into the individual's daily life and routine.

Person-centered planning also involves a commitment to ongoing monitoring and evaluation of the individual's progress and outcomes. This may involve regular check-ins with the individual and their support network, as well as the use of objective data collection and analysis to track changes in behavior and to make adjustments to the intervention plan as needed. By taking a dynamic and responsive approach, practitioners can help to ensure that interventions remain relevant and effective over time.

In the context of adult ID/DD high-risk forensic individuals, person-centered planning may also involve a recognition of the unique challenges and risks associated with criminal justice involvement. This may include addressing issues such as substance abuse, mental health concerns, or a history of trauma or victimization, and developing interventions that are tailored to the individual's specific needs and circumstances.

Person-centered planning may also involve collaboration with criminal justice professionals, such as probation officers or court personnel, to ensure that behavioral interventions are aligned with legal requirements and public safety concerns. This may involve developing individualized risk management plans or advocating for alternative sentencing or diversion programs that prioritize rehabilitation and community-based support.

Ultimately, the goal of person-centered planning and support is to promote greater self-determination, independence, and quality of life for adult ID/DD high-risk forensic individuals. By recognizing the individual's unique strengths, needs, and preferences, and by involving them as active participants in the planning and implementation of services, practitioners can help to create more effective and sustainable interventions that support the individual's long-term success and well-being.

C. Collaborative approaches with multidisciplinary teams

Collaborative approaches with multidisciplinary teams are essential for providing comprehensive and effective support to adult ID/DD high-risk forensic individuals.

These teams may include a range of professionals from different disciplines, such as behavior analysts, psychologists, social workers, occupational therapists, and criminal justice professionals, who work together to address the complex needs of this population.

One of the key benefits of multidisciplinary collaboration is the ability to draw upon a diverse range of expertise and perspectives. Each member of the team brings a unique set of knowledge, skills, and experiences that can contribute to a more holistic understanding of the individual's needs and challenges. By working together, team members can develop a more comprehensive and integrated approach to intervention that addresses multiple domains of functioning, such as cognitive, social, emotional, and behavioral.

Multidisciplinary collaboration also allows for greater coordination and continuity of care across different settings and systems. Adult ID/DD high-risk forensic individuals may be involved with multiple service providers and agencies, such as mental health clinics, vocational rehabilitation programs, and criminal justice agencies. By working together as a team, professionals can help to ensure that interventions are consistent and complementary and that there is a seamless transition of care between different settings.

Another important aspect of multidisciplinary collaboration is the ability to share information and resources across different disciplines. This may involve sharing assessment data, treatment plans, and progress reports, as well as identifying and leveraging community resources and supports that can enhance the individual's functioning and quality of life. By working together, team members can help to ensure that interventions are comprehensive, efficient, and effective.

Multidisciplinary collaboration also allows for greater accountability and oversight in the provision of services. By involving multiple professionals in the planning and implementation of interventions, there is a greater likelihood of identifying and addressing potential problems or challenges early on, and of ensuring that interventions are being delivered with fidelity and integrity.

In the context of adult ID/DD high-risk forensic individuals, multidisciplinary collaboration may also involve working closely with criminal justice professionals, such as probation officers, judges, and attorneys. These professionals can provide valuable insights into the individual's legal status and requirements, as well as help to ensure that interventions are aligned with public safety concerns and community standards.

Multidisciplinary collaboration may also involve working with family members and other natural supports, who can provide valuable information about the individual's history, preferences, and daily life experiences. By involving family members and other supports in the planning and implementation of interventions, professionals can help to ensure that interventions are culturally responsive and socially valid and that they are integrated into the individual's natural environment.

To facilitate effective multidisciplinary collaboration, it is important to establish clear roles, responsibilities, and communication channels among team members. This may involve regular team meetings, case conferences, and progress reviews, as well as the use of shared documentation and data management systems. It may also involve providing training and support to team members to ensure that they have the knowledge and skills needed to work effectively with this population.

Ultimately, the goal of multidisciplinary collaboration is to provide the most comprehensive and effective support possible to adult ID/DD high-risk forensic individuals. By working together as a team, professionals can help to address the complex needs of this population, promote positive outcomes, and enhance their overall quality of life. This requires a commitment to ongoing communication, coordination, and collaboration, as well as a willingness to adapt and innovate in response to the changing needs and circumstances of the individuals served.

A. Conducting comprehensive assessments (e.g., adaptive behavior, cognitive functioning, risk factors)

Conducting comprehensive assessments is a critical component of providing effective support to adult ID/DD high-risk forensic individuals. These assessments should be multidimensional and tailored to the specific needs and characteristics of the individual and should cover a range of domains, including adaptive behavior, cognitive functioning, and risk factors.

Adaptive behavior assessments are designed to evaluate an individual's ability to function independently in everyday life activities, such as self-care, communication, social skills, and community living. These assessments may involve a combination of standardized tests, such as the Vineland Adaptive Behavior Scales, as well as interviews with the individual and their caregivers, and direct observation of the individual's behavior in natural settings. The results of these assessments can help to identify areas of strength and weakness in the individual's adaptive functioning and can inform the development of individualized support plans that target specific skill deficits.

Cognitive functioning assessments are designed to evaluate an individual's intellectual abilities, such as their verbal and nonverbal reasoning, memory, attention, and processing speed. These assessments may involve the use of standardized intelligence tests, such as the Wechsler Adult Intelligence Scale or the Stanford-Binet Intelligence Scales, as well as neuropsychological tests that assess specific cognitive domains. The results of these assessments can help to identify the individual's cognitive strengths and limitations and can inform the selection of appropriate interventions and supports.

Risk assessments are designed to evaluate an individual's likelihood of engaging in future criminal behavior, as well as the factors that may contribute to their risk. These assessments may involve the use of standardized risk assessment tools, such as the Level of Service Inventory-Revised or the Historical Clinical Risk Management-20, as well as a review of the individual's criminal history, mental health history, and other relevant background information. The results of these assessments can help to identify specific risk factors that may need to be addressed through targeted interventions, such as substance abuse treatment or anger management training.

In addition to these core assessments, comprehensive evaluations of adult ID/DD high-risk forensic individuals may also include assessments of other relevant domains, such as mental health functioning, trauma history, and social support networks. These assessments can help to provide a more holistic understanding of the individual's needs and challenges and can inform the development of comprehensive treatment plans that address multiple areas of functioning.

It is important to note that assessments of adult ID/DD high-risk forensic individuals should be conducted using culturally and linguistically appropriate measures, and should take into account the individual's unique background and experiences. Assessors should also be mindful of the potential for bias and should strive to use objective and evidence-based assessment methods whenever possible.

Finally, assessments of adult ID/DD high-risk forensic individuals should be conducted as part of an ongoing process of evaluation and monitoring, rather than as a one-time event. Regular reassessments can help to track the individual's progress over time, identify emerging needs or challenges, and adjust interventions as needed to ensure that they remain effective and relevant.

B. Identifying target behaviors and their functions

Identifying target behaviors and their functions is a key step in developing effective behavioral interventions for adult ID/DD high-risk forensic individuals. Target behaviors are specific, observable actions that are of concern or that interfere with the individual's functioning, such as aggression, self-injury, or substance abuse. Functions refer to the underlying reasons or purposes that the behavior serves for the individual, such as gaining attention, escaping demands, or accessing tangible rewards.

To identify target behaviors and their functions, practitioners may use a variety of assessment methods, including:

1. Direct observation: This involves systematically observing the individual's behavior in natural settings, such as at home, work, or in the community. Observers may use standardized recording methods, such as frequency counts or duration recording, to quantify the occurrence of target behaviors and to identify patterns or triggers.

2. Functional analysis: This involves systematically manipulating environmental variables to identify the specific conditions under which target behaviors are more or less likely to occur. For example, a practitioner may withhold attention or present demands to see if the individual's behavior changes in response to these conditions.

3. Interviews: This involves gathering information from the individual and their caregivers about the target behaviors, including when and where they occur, what precedes or follows them, and what the individual may be trying to communicate or achieve through the behavior.

4. Rating scales: This involves using standardized questionnaires or checklists to assess the frequency, intensity, and duration of target behaviors, as well as the impact that they have on the individual's functioning and quality of life.

Once target behaviors and their functions have been identified, practitioners can use this information to develop individualized behavior support plans that address the specific needs and challenges of the individual. These plans may include a range of strategies, such as:

1. **Antecedent interventions**: These involve modifying the environment or the individual's routine to prevent or reduce the likelihood of target behaviors occurring. For example, providing visual schedules or reducing noise levels may help to reduce anxiety and prevent outbursts.

2. **Skill-building interventions**: These involve teaching the individual new skills or behaviors that can serve as alternatives to the target behaviors. For example, teaching communication skills or coping strategies may help the individual to express their needs or manage their emotions in more appropriate ways.

3. **Consequence interventions**: These involve providing positive or negative consequences for the individual's behavior, depending on whether the behavior is desired or undesired. For example, providing praise or rewards for appropriate

behavior, or withholding attention for inappropriate behavior, can help to shape the individual's behavior over time.

It is important to note that behavior support plans should be individualized and tailored to the specific needs and preferences of the individual. They should also be developed in collaboration with the individual and their support network and should be regularly reviewed and revised based on data and feedback.

Finally, behavior support plans should be implemented consistently and with fidelity across all settings and caregivers. This requires ongoing training and support for staff and family members, as well as regular monitoring and evaluation to ensure that the plan is effective and sustainable over time.

C. Developing individualized support plans

Developing individualized support plans is a critical component of providing effective support to adult ID/DD high-risk forensic individuals. These plans should be comprehensive, person-centered, and tailored to the specific needs, strengths, and goals of the individual.

The process of developing an individualized support plan typically involves the following steps:

1. **Assessment**: As discussed earlier, the first step in developing an individualized support plan is to conduct a comprehensive assessment of the individual's needs, strengths, and challenges. This may include assessments of adaptive behavior, cognitive functioning, mental health, and risk factors, as well as input from the individual and their support network.

2. **Goal setting**: Based on the results of the assessment, the next step is to identify specific, measurable goals that the individual wants to achieve. These goals should be realistic, achievable, and aligned with the individual's values and preferences. They may include goals related to skill development, behavior change, community integration, or other areas of functioning.

3. **Intervention planning**: Once goals have been identified, the next step is to develop a plan for achieving those goals. This may involve selecting evidence-based interventions or strategies that are effective for individuals with similar needs and challenges. Interventions may include behavioral interventions, such as those

described earlier, as well as other types of support, such as counseling, medication management, or vocational training.

4. Resource identification: Developing an effective individualized support plan also requires identifying and securing the necessary resources and support to implement the plan. This may include identifying funding sources, such as Medicaid or state waiver programs, as well as identifying community-based resources, such as housing, transportation, or employment services.

5. Implementation: Once the plan has been developed and resources have been secured, the next step is to implement the plan. This may involve training staff or caregivers on the specific interventions or strategies included in the plan, as well as establishing clear roles and responsibilities for each member of the support team.

6. Monitoring and evaluation: Finally, individualized support plans should be regularly monitored and evaluated to ensure that they are effective and that the individual is making progress toward their goals. This may involve collecting data on the individual's behavior, skills, or other outcomes, as well as soliciting feedback from the individual and their support network.

Individualized support plans should be developed using a person-centered approach, which means that the individual should be actively involved in the planning process and should have a voice in determining their own goals and preferences. This may involve using alternative communication methods, such as visual supports or assistive technology, to ensure that the individual can fully participate in the planning process.

Individualized support plans should also be culturally responsive and should take into account the individual's unique background, experiences, and values. This may involve incorporating culturally specific interventions or supports or involving family members or other cultural brokers in the planning process.

In addition, individualized support plans should be flexible and adaptable, and should be regularly reviewed and revised based on the individual's changing needs and circumstances. This may involve modifying interventions or supports as needed or identifying new goals or priorities as the individual progresses or encounters new challenges.

Finally, individualized support plans should be developed and implemented using a collaborative, multidisciplinary approach, as described earlier. This means involving a range of professionals and stakeholders in the planning process, including behavior analysts, psychologists, social workers, and criminal justice professionals, as well as the individual and their support network. By working together as a team, professionals can ensure that the plan is comprehensive, coordinated, and effective in meeting the individual's unique needs and goals.

Chapter V. Behavioral Intervention Strategies for ID/DD High-Risk Forensic Adults

A. Positive behavior support (PBS) strategies

Positive behavior support (PBS) is a comprehensive, evidence-based approach to addressing challenging behaviors in individuals with intellectual and developmental disabilities (ID/DD), including those who are at high risk for involvement in the criminal justice system. PBS focuses on understanding the underlying reasons for challenging behaviors and developing proactive strategies to prevent or reduce their occurrence, while also teaching and reinforcing positive, prosocial behaviors.

The key principles of PBS include:

1. Conducting a functional behavior assessment (FBA) to identify the antecedents, consequences, and functions of challenging behaviors.

2. Develop a behavior support plan that includes proactive strategies to prevent challenging behaviors, as well as reactive strategies to respond effectively when they do occur.

3. Teaching and reinforcing positive replacement behaviors that serve the same function as the challenging behavior, but are more socially appropriate and effective.

4. Modifying the environment and providing necessary support and accommodations to promote success and reduce the likelihood of challenging behaviors.

5. Involving the individual and their support network in the development and implementation of the behavior support plan, and ensuring that the plan is culturally responsive and person-centered.

PBS strategies may include a range of interventions, such as:

1. **Antecedent interventions**: These involve identifying and modifying the triggers or situations that are likely to lead to challenging behaviors. For example, providing visual schedules, reducing noise levels, or offering choices may help to reduce anxiety and prevent outbursts.

2. **Skill-building interventions**: These involve teaching the individual new skills or behaviors that can serve as alternatives to challenging behaviors. For example,

teaching communication skills, coping strategies, or social skills may help the individual to express their needs or manage their emotions in more appropriate ways.

3. **Reinforcement interventions:** These involve providing positive reinforcement for appropriate behaviors, such as praise, rewards, or access to preferred activities. Reinforcement should be individualized and meaningful to the individual and should be provided consistently and contingently.

4. **Crisis management interventions:** These involve developing a plan for responding effectively to crises, such as aggression or self-injury. The plan should include strategies for de-escalation, as well as protocols for ensuring the safety of the individual and others.

PBS strategies should be individualized and tailored to the specific needs and preferences of the individual and should be implemented consistently across all settings and caregivers. Regular monitoring and evaluation of the effectiveness of the interventions is also important, and the behavior support plan should be revised as needed based on data and feedback.

B. Functional communication training (FCT)

Functional communication training (FCT) is a specific type of PBS intervention that focuses on teaching individuals with ID/DD to communicate their needs and desires in more appropriate and effective ways, rather than engaging in challenging behaviors to get their needs met.

The basic premise of FCT is that challenging behaviors often serve a communicative function, such as gaining attention, escaping demands, or accessing tangible items. By teaching the individual an alternative way to communicate those needs, such as using verbal requests, gestures, or picture exchange systems, the challenging behavior may become less necessary or effective.

The process of implementing FCT typically involves the following steps:

1. Conducting an FBA to identify the communicative function of the challenging behavior.

2. Selecting an appropriate communication modality based on the individual's skills and preferences, such as verbal language, sign language, or augmentative and alternative communication (AAC) devices.

3. Teaching the individual to use the communication modality to request the desired item or activity, using prompting and reinforcement strategies.

4. Gradually fading the prompts and reinforcing the independent use of the communication skill in natural contexts.

5. Monitoring the effectiveness of the intervention and adjusting as needed based on data and feedback.

FCT is an effective intervention for reducing challenging behaviors and increasing functional communication skills in individuals with ID/DD, including those who are at high risk for involvement in the criminal justice system. However, it is important to note that FCT should be implemented as part of a comprehensive behavior support plan that also addresses other factors that may be contributing to the challenging behavior, such as environmental triggers or skill deficits.

C. Teaching replacement behaviors and coping skills

Teaching replacement behaviors and coping skills is another important component of behavioral intervention for individuals with ID/DD who are at high risk for involvement in the criminal justice system. Replacement behaviors are alternative behaviors that serve the same function as the challenging behavior but are more socially appropriate and effective. Coping skills are strategies that individuals can use to manage their emotions and stress in challenging situations.

The process of teaching replacement behaviors and coping skills typically involves the following steps:

1. Identifying the function of the challenging behavior through an FBA.

2. Selecting an appropriate replacement behavior or coping skill based on the individual's skills, preferences, and the context in which the challenging behavior occurs.

3. Teaching the individual the replacement behavior or coping skill using modeling, role-playing, and other instructional strategies.

4. Providing opportunities for the individual to practice the new skill in a variety of contexts, with prompting and feedback as needed.

5. Reinforcing the use of the replacement behavior or coping skill in natural contexts, and gradually fading the reinforcement as the skill becomes more established.

Examples of replacement behaviors and coping skills that may be taught to individuals with ID/DD who are at high risk for involvement in the criminal justice system include:

1. Asking for a break or a change in activity when feeling overwhelmed or frustrated, instead of engaging in aggressive or disruptive behavior.

2. Using deep breathing, progressive muscle relaxation, or other relaxation techniques to manage anxiety or stress.

3. Seeking out social support or engaging in positive self-talk when facing a challenging situation.

4. Using problem-solving skills to identify and evaluate potential solutions to conflicts or challenges.

It is important to note that the selection and teaching of replacement behaviors and coping skills should be individualized and based on a thorough assessment of the individual's needs, strengths, and challenges. The skills should also be taught in a way that is developmentally appropriate and culturally responsive and should be practiced and reinforced in a variety of contexts to promote generalization and maintenance.

D. Addressing specific challenges (e.g., aggression, self-injurious behavior, sexual offending)

Individuals with ID/DD who are at high risk for involvement in the criminal justice system may present with a range of specific challenges, such as aggression, self-injurious behavior, or sexual offending. These challenges require specialized assessment and intervention strategies that are tailored to the unique needs and risk factors of the individual.

Aggression is a common challenge among individuals with ID/DD and may take the form of physical aggression towards others, property destruction, or verbal threats. The first step in addressing aggression is to conduct an FBA to identify the triggers and functions of the behavior. Based on this assessment, a comprehensive behavior support plan can be developed that includes proactive strategies to prevent aggression, such as modifying the environment or teaching coping skills, as well as reactive strategies to respond effectively when aggression does occur, such as using de-escalation techniques or implementing safety protocols.

Self-injurious behavior (SIB) is another significant challenge that may occur among individuals with ID/DD and involves the intentional infliction of physical harm to oneself, such as head-banging, biting, or scratching. Like aggression, SIB requires a thorough FBA to identify the underlying functions of the behavior, which may include sensory stimulation, escape from demands, or access to attention. Treatment for SIB may involve a combination of medical interventions to address any underlying health issues, as well as behavioral interventions to teach alternative coping strategies and reinforce positive behaviors.

Sexual offending is a particularly complex challenge that may occur among a small subset of individuals with ID/DD and requires specialized assessment and treatment approaches. Risk factors for sexual offending may include a history of sexual abuse or trauma, poor social skills or boundaries, and limited sexual knowledge or education. Treatment for sexual offending typically involves a comprehensive approach that includes cognitive-behavioral therapy, sex education, and relapse prevention strategies, as well as close collaboration with criminal justice and community supervision agencies.

Across all of these specific challenges, it is important to use evidence-based, trauma-sensitive, and culturally responsive interventions that are tailored to the unique needs and strengths of the individual. This may involve adapting traditional behavioral interventions to be more accessible or effective for individuals with ID/DD, such as using visual supports or simplified language. It may also involve collaborating closely with other professionals and stakeholders, such as mental health providers, medical professionals, and criminal justice agencies, to ensure a coordinated and comprehensive approach to treatment.

E. Incorporating visual supports and accommodations

Incorporating visual supports and accommodations is an important strategy for promoting the success and independence of individuals with ID/DD who are at high risk for involvement in the criminal justice system. Visual supports are tools that use pictures, symbols, or other visual cues to enhance communication, understanding, and learning. Accommodations are modifications or adaptations to the environment, materials, or instruction that are designed to meet the unique needs and abilities of the individual.

Many different types of visual supports and accommodations can be used to support individuals with ID/DD, depending on their specific needs and challenges. Some examples include:

1. **Visual schedules:** These are visual representations of the activities or tasks that an individual needs to complete throughout the day, using pictures, symbols, or words. Visual schedules can help to provide structure and predictability, reduce anxiety, and promote independence.

2. **Social stories**: These are short, simple stories that describe a particular social situation or skill, using a combination of text and pictures. Social stories can help individuals understand and navigate social expectations and norms and can be used to teach specific social skills or behaviors.

3. **Communication boards or devices:** These are tools that allow individuals to express their needs, wants, or thoughts using pictures, symbols, or voice output.

Communication boards or devices can be low-tech, such as a picture exchange system, or high-tech, such as a speech-generating device.

4. Visual cues or prompts: These are visual reminders or signals that help individuals initiate or complete a particular behavior or task. Examples might include a picture of a raised hand to prompt the individual to ask for help, or a color-coded system to indicate the steps in a task.

5. Environmental modifications: These are changes to the physical environment that are designed to reduce distractions, promote safety, or enhance accessibility. Examples might include using noise-cancelling headphones, providing a quiet space for breaks, or installing grab bars in the bathroom.

When incorporating visual supports and accommodations, it is important to consider the individual's specific needs, preferences, and abilities. The supports and accommodations should be tailored to the individual and should be implemented consistently across settings and caregivers. It is also important to provide training and support to staff and family members on how to use the supports and accommodations effectively.

In addition to promoting success and independence, visual supports and accommodations can also help to reduce the likelihood of challenging behaviors and promote positive interactions with others. For example, using a communication board to express needs and wants may reduce frustration and aggression, while using social stories to teach appropriate social behaviors may improve social relationships and reduce the risk of offending.

Overall, incorporating visual supports and accommodations is an essential component of providing effective behavioral intervention and support for individuals with ID/DD who are at high risk for involvement in the criminal justice system. By using these strategies in combination with other evidence-based practices, such as positive behavior support and functional communication training, practitioners can help to promote the success, independence, and well-being of this vulnerable population.

<u>Chapter VI. Promoting Community Integration and Positive Outcomes</u>

<u>A. Strategies for increasing independence and self-determination</u>

Promoting independence and self-determination is a critical goal for individuals with ID/DD who are at high risk for involvement in the criminal justice system. Independence refers to the ability to perform daily living skills and make decisions without relying on others for assistance, while self-determination refers to the ability to make choices and direct one's own life based on personal preferences, values, and goals.

Several strategies can be used to promote independence and self-determination for individuals with ID/DD, including:

1. **Person-centered planning:** This involves working collaboratively with the individual and their support network to identify their strengths, interests, and goals, and developing a plan to achieve those goals. Person-centered planning emphasizes the individual's autonomy and choices and involves them as an active participant in the decision-making process.

2. Skill-building: Teaching and reinforcing daily living skills, such as personal hygiene, meal preparation, and money management, can help individuals become more independent in their daily lives. Skill-building should be individualized and based on the individual's specific needs and abilities and should involve a gradual process of teaching, modeling, and fading support.

3. Assistive technology: The use of assistive technology, such as communication devices, visual schedules, or smart home technology, can help individuals perform tasks and make decisions more independently. Assistive technology should be selected based on the individual's specific needs and preferences and should be accompanied by training and support for the individual and their caregivers.

4. Choice-making opportunities: Providing opportunities for individuals to make choices and express preferences, such as choosing their meals, activities, or living arrangements, can help to promote self-determination and autonomy. Choice-making should be built into daily routines and interactions and should be accompanied by education and support to help individuals understand the consequences and responsibilities of their choices.

5. Self-advocacy: Encouraging and supporting individuals to speak up for themselves and advocate for their needs and rights can help to promote self-determination and empowerment. Self-advocacy can be taught through role-playing, social stories, or peer support groups, and should be reinforced through positive feedback and recognition.

Promoting independence and self-determination requires a shift in the way that support is provided to individuals with ID/DD, from a model of care and protection to a model of empowerment and self-direction. This shift requires buy-in and collaboration from all members of the individual's support network, including family members, caregivers, and professionals. It also requires ongoing assessment and adjustment to ensure that the individual's needs and preferences are being met and that they are making progress towards their goals.

B. Developing social skills and relationships

Developing social skills and relationships is another critical component of promoting community integration and positive outcomes for individuals with ID/DD who are at high risk for involvement in the criminal justice system. Social skills refer to the ability to interact effectively with others, while relationships refer to the positive connections and attachments that individuals form with others in their social network.

Several strategies can be used to promote the development of social skills and relationships for individuals with ID/DD, including:

1. **Social skills training:** This involves explicitly teaching and practicing specific social skills, such as initiating conversations, taking turns, or resolving conflicts. Social skills training can be delivered through individual or group sessions and should be tailored to the individual's specific needs and abilities. Training should involve a combination of instruction, modeling, role-playing, and feedback, and should be reinforced through real-world practice and positive reinforcement.

2. **Peer support**: Connecting individuals with ID/DD to peers who have similar experiences and challenges can provide a sense of belonging and support, and can help to promote the development of positive relationships. Peer support can be facilitated through structured programs, such as social clubs or mentoring relationships, or through informal connections and activities.

3. Community involvement: Encouraging and supporting individuals with ID/DD to participate in community activities and events can provide opportunities for social interaction and relationship-building. Community involvement can be facilitated through partnerships with local organizations, such as churches, community centers, or advocacy groups, and should be based on the individual's interests and preferences.

4. Technology-based interventions: The use of technology, such as social media, video modeling, or virtual reality, can provide additional opportunities for individuals with ID/DD to practice and develop social skills in a safe and controlled environment. Technology-based interventions should be selected based on the individual's specific needs and abilities and should be accompanied by training and support for the individual and their caregivers.

5. Family and caregiver involvement: Involving family members and caregivers in the development and reinforcement of social skills and relationships can help to promote generalization and maintenance of these skills across settings. Family and caregiver involvement can be facilitated through education and training, as well as through opportunities for joint activities and experiences.

Developing social skills and relationships requires a comprehensive and individualized approach that takes into account the unique strengths, needs, and preferences of each individual with ID/DD. It also requires ongoing assessment and adjustment to ensure that the individual is making progress and that their social network is providing the necessary support and encouragement.

C. Vocational training and supported employment

Vocational training and supported employment are important strategies for promoting community integration and positive outcomes for individuals with ID/DD who are at high risk for involvement in the criminal justice system. Vocational training refers to the acquisition of job-specific skills and knowledge, while supported employment refers to the provision of ongoing support and accommodations to help individuals maintain competitive employment in the community.

There are several key components of effective vocational training and supported employment for individuals with ID/DD, including:

1. **Person-centered planning**: Vocational goals and preferences should be identified through a collaborative process that involves the individual, their family members, and their support team. Person-centered planning should take into account the individual's strengths, interests, and abilities, as well as any barriers or challenges that may impact their employment success.

2. **Job development**: Once vocational goals have been identified, job development activities should be undertaken to identify potential employment opportunities that match the individual's skills and interests. Job development may involve networking with local businesses, attending job fairs, or working with employment agencies or vocational rehabilitation services.

3. **Job coaching and support**: Individuals with ID/DD may require ongoing support and coaching to learn and maintain job skills, as well as to navigate the social and cultural aspects of the workplace. Job coaching may involve on-the-job training, problem-solving assistance, and communication with employers and co-workers. Support may also be provided to help individuals manage stress, resolve conflicts, or advocate for accommodations or modifications to the work environment.

4. Customized employment: For individuals with more significant support needs, customized employment may be an effective approach. Customized employment involves negotiating job duties and responsibilities that are tailored to the individual's specific strengths and interests, and may involve job carving, job sharing, or self-employment options.

5. Benefits planning: Individuals with ID/DD who receive public benefits, such as Supplemental Security Income (SSI) or Medicaid, may face barriers to employment due to concerns about losing eligibility for these benefits. Benefits planning involves working with individuals and their families to understand the impact of employment on benefits, and to develop strategies for maximizing income while maintaining necessary supports and services.

Vocational training and supported employment can provide individuals with ID/DD with opportunities for meaningful work, social connections, and increased independence and self-sufficiency. These opportunities can also help to reduce the risk of criminal justice involvement by providing structure, purpose, and positive reinforcement for prosocial behaviors.

However, the success of vocational training and supported employment for individuals with ID/DD who are at high risk for involvement in the criminal justice system may depend on several factors, including:

- The availability of appropriate job opportunities in the local community

- The willingness of employers to provide accommodations and support for individuals with disabilities

- The coordination and collaboration among different service systems, including vocational rehabilitation, mental health, and criminal justice agencies

- The availability of ongoing funding and resources for job coaching and support services

Addressing these systemic barriers may require advocacy and policy change at the local, state, and national levels, as well as increased public awareness and education about the benefits of employment for individuals with disabilities.

<u>**D. Collaborating with community resources and support systems**</u>

Collaborating with community resources and support systems is essential for promoting community integration and positive outcomes for individuals with ID/DD who are at high risk for involvement in the criminal justice system. Community resources and support systems can provide a range of services and support that can help individuals live independently, develop social connections, and access necessary healthcare and other services.

There are several key strategies for collaborating with community resources and support systems, including:

1. **Identifying and mapping community resources:** The first step in collaborating with community resources is to identify what resources are available in the local community, and to develop a comprehensive resource map that includes contact information, eligibility criteria, and referral processes. This resource map should be shared with all members of the individual's support team, including family members, caregivers, and service providers.

2. Developing partnerships and memorandums of understanding (MOUs):
Formal partnerships and MOUs can help to establish clear roles, responsibilities, and communication protocols among different community agencies and service providers. These agreements can help to ensure that individuals with ID/DD receive coordinated and comprehensive services, and can help to prevent duplication or gaps in service delivery.

3. Engaging in cross-system training and education: Cross-system training and education can help to build shared understanding and expertise among different service providers and community partners. This may involve joint training sessions, case consultations, or other opportunities for service providers to learn about each other's roles, responsibilities, and approaches to supporting individuals with ID/DD.

4. Involving individuals and families in service planning and delivery:
Individuals with ID/DD and their family members should be actively involved in the planning and delivery of community-based services and supports. This may involve person-centered planning processes, family education and support programs, or peer support and advocacy groups.

5. Advocating for system and policy change: Collaborating with community resources and support systems may also involve advocating for system and policy changes that can improve access to and coordination of services for individuals with ID/DD. This may involve working with local, state, or national advocacy organizations to promote increased funding, regulatory changes, or other reforms that can support community integration and positive outcomes.

Some examples of community resources and support systems that may be important for individuals with ID/DD who are at high risk for involvement in the criminal justice system include:

- Mental health and substance abuse treatment services

- Housing and residential support services

- Transportation and mobility services

- Assistive technology and adaptive equipment providers

- Social and recreational programs and activities

- Faith-based and cultural organizations

- Advocacy and self-help groups

Collaborating with these and other community resources and support systems can help to create a more comprehensive and coordinated system of care for individuals with ID/DD, and can help to prevent or mitigate the negative outcomes associated with criminal justice involvement. However, effective collaboration requires ongoing communication, trust-building, and a shared commitment to person-centered and strengths-based approaches to support and service delivery.

Chapter VII. Legal and Ethical Considerations

A. Informed consent and capacity to make decisions

Informed consent and capacity to make decisions are critical legal and ethical considerations when working with individuals with ID/DD who are at high risk for involvement in the criminal justice system. Informed consent refers to the process of providing individuals with clear and comprehensive information about proposed interventions or services, and obtaining their voluntary agreement to participate. The capacity to make decisions refers to an individual's ability to understand and appreciate the nature and consequences of a particular decision and to communicate a choice based on that understanding.

There are several key principles and strategies for addressing informed consent and the capacity to make decisions when working with individuals with ID/DD, including:

1. **Presuming competence:** Individuals with ID/DD should be presumed to have the capacity to make decisions about their own lives unless there is clear evidence to the contrary. This presumption of competence is essential for promoting self-

determination and autonomy, and for avoiding unnecessary restrictions on individual rights and freedoms.

2. Providing accommodations and support: Individuals with ID/DD may require accommodations and support to participate meaningfully in the informed consent process, and to make decisions about their care and treatment. This may involve using plain language, visual aids, or other communication supports, as well as providing additional time and opportunities for questions and discussion.

3. Assessing capacity on a decision-specific basis: The capacity to make decisions should be assessed on a decision-specific basis, rather than globally. This means that an individual may have the capacity to make some decisions but not others, depending on the complexity and consequences of the decision at hand. Capacity assessments should be conducted by trained professionals, using standardized tools and protocols.

4. Involving surrogate decision-makers when necessary: When an individual with ID/DD is found to lack the capacity to make a particular decision, a surrogate decision-maker may need to be appointed to make decisions on their behalf.

Surrogate decision-makers may include family members, legal guardians, or other individuals who are familiar with the individual's values, preferences, and best interests.

5. Balancing autonomy and protection: There may be situations where an individual with ID/DD is at risk of harm to themselves or others, and where their autonomy needs to be balanced against concerns for their safety and well-being. In these situations, professionals may need to use the least restrictive interventions possible, and to involve the individual and their support network in the decision-making process to the greatest extent possible.

Informed consent and capacity to make decisions are particularly important considerations in the context of the criminal justice system, where individuals with ID/DD may be at risk of waiving their legal rights or accepting plea bargains without fully understanding the consequences. Professionals working in these contexts may need to take additional steps to ensure that individuals with ID/DD are fully informed and supported in their decision-making and that their legal rights are protected throughout the criminal justice process.

Balancing individual rights and public safety is another critical legal and ethical consideration when working with individuals with ID/DD who are at high risk for involvement in the criminal justice system. On one hand, individuals with ID/DD have the same basic human rights as anyone else, including the right to liberty, autonomy, and self-determination. On the other hand, there may be situations where an individual's behavior poses a significant risk of harm to themselves or others, and where their rights need to be balanced against the need to protect public safety.

There are several key principles and strategies for balancing individual rights and public safety when working with individuals with ID/DD, including:

1. **Using the least restrictive interventions possible:** When an individual with ID/DD is at risk of harm to themselves or others, professionals should use the least restrictive interventions possible to mitigate that risk. This may involve using positive behavior support strategies, crisis intervention techniques, or other evidence-based approaches that prioritize the individual's safety and well-being while minimizing the use of coercion or control.

2. Conducting comprehensive risk assessments: Comprehensive risk assessments can help professionals to identify the specific factors that may be contributing to an individual's risk of harm, and to develop targeted interventions to address those factors. Risk assessments should be conducted using standardized tools and protocols, and should take into account the individual's unique strengths, needs, and circumstances.

3. Collaborating with criminal justice and mental health systems: Balancing individual rights and public safety may require close collaboration and coordination between criminal justice and mental health systems. This may involve developing specialized court programs, diversion initiatives, or other interventions that provide individuals with ID/DD with access to necessary support and services while also ensuring accountability and public safety.

4. Promoting community-based alternatives to incarceration: Incarceration can be particularly harmful for individuals with ID/DD, who may be more vulnerable to victimization, exploitation, and other negative outcomes in correctional settings. Promoting community-based alternatives to incarceration, such as supported housing, vocational training, and mental health treatment, can help to reduce the risk of recidivism while also supporting the individual's overall well-being and quality of life.

5. Engaging in ongoing monitoring and evaluation: Balancing individual rights and public safety requires ongoing monitoring and evaluation to ensure that interventions are effective, appropriate, and responsive to the individual's changing needs and circumstances. This may involve regular check-ins with the individual and their support network, as well as data collection and analysis to track progress and outcomes over time.

Ultimately, balancing individual rights and public safety when working with individuals with ID/DD who are at high risk for involvement in the criminal justice system requires a nuanced and individualized approach that takes into account the unique factors and circumstances of each case. Professionals working in these contexts must be willing to engage in difficult conversations and ethical decision-making and to prioritize the individual's well-being and autonomy to the greatest extent possible while also ensuring the safety and security of the broader community.

C. Navigating the criminal justice system

Navigating the criminal justice system can be a complex and challenging process for individuals with ID/DD who are at high risk for involvement in this system. Individuals with ID/DD may face a range of barriers and challenges at every stage of the criminal justice process, from initial contact with law enforcement to sentencing and post-incarceration support.

There are several key strategies and considerations for navigating the criminal justice system when working with individuals with ID/DD, including:

1. Providing education and training for criminal justice professionals: Criminal justice professionals, including law enforcement officers, attorneys, and judges, may lack knowledge and understanding of the unique needs and challenges faced by individuals with ID/DD. Providing education and training on topics such as effective communication strategies, behavior support techniques, and risk assessment can help to improve the responsiveness and appropriateness of the criminal justice system for this population.

2. Advocating for specialized court programs and diversion initiatives:
Specialized court programs and diversion initiatives, such as mental health courts or drug courts, can provide individuals with ID/DD with access to necessary support and services while also ensuring accountability and public safety. Advocating for the development and expansion of these programs can help to reduce the overrepresentation of individuals with ID/DD in the criminal justice system.

3. Ensuring access to legal representation and advocacy: Individuals with ID/DD may face significant barriers to accessing legal representation and advocacy services, which can impact their ability to navigate the criminal justice system effectively. Ensuring that individuals with ID/DD have access to trained and experienced legal professionals who can provide them with the support and advocacy they need can help to protect their legal rights and ensure a fair and just outcome.

4. Providing support and accommodations throughout the criminal justice process: Individuals with ID/DD may require a range of supports and accommodations throughout the criminal justice process, from communication aids and visual supports to modified sentencing options and post-incarceration support services. Providing these supports and accommodations can help to ensure that individuals with ID/DD can participate fully and meaningfully in the criminal justice process.

5. Collaborating with community-based organizations and support systems: Navigating the criminal justice system often requires close collaboration and coordination with community-based organizations and support systems, such as mental health providers, housing agencies, and vocational rehabilitation services. Building strong partnerships and referral networks can help to ensure that individuals with ID/DD receive the comprehensive and coordinated support they need to successfully reintegrate into the community and avoid future involvement with the criminal justice system.

Navigating the criminal justice system when working with individuals with ID/DD requires a multidisciplinary and collaborative approach that prioritizes the individual's unique needs and circumstances. Professionals working in these contexts must be willing to advocate for the rights and well-being of individuals with ID/DD, while also ensuring the safety and security of the broader community.

By providing education, support, and advocacy at every stage of the criminal justice process, professionals can help to promote a more just and equitable system for individuals with ID/DD who are at high risk for involvement in this system.

D. Advocacy and policy implications

Advocacy and policy change are critical components of promoting the rights and well-being of individuals with ID/DD who are at high risk for involvement in the criminal justice system. Despite growing recognition of the unique needs and challenges faced by this population, many individuals with ID/DD continue to experience significant barriers and disparities in access to necessary supports and services, both within and outside of the criminal justice system.

There are several key strategies and considerations for advocacy and policy change when working with individuals with ID/DD who are at high risk for involvement in the criminal justice system, including:

1. Promoting inclusive and accessible communities: Advocacy efforts should focus on promoting inclusive and accessible communities that provide individuals with ID/DD with the support and opportunities they need to live full and meaningful lives. This may involve advocating for increased funding for community-based services and supports, such as supported housing, employment, and mental health treatment, as well as promoting greater awareness and understanding of the rights and needs of individuals with ID/DD.

2. **Reforming the criminal justice system**: Advocacy efforts should also focus on reforming the criminal justice system to better meet the needs of individuals with ID/DD. This may involve advocating for the development and expansion of specialized court programs and diversion initiatives, as well as promoting training and education for criminal justice professionals on the unique needs and challenges faced by this population.

3. **Ensuring access to legal representation and advocacy**: Ensuring that individuals with ID/DD have access to trained and experienced legal professionals who can provide them with the support and advocacy they need is critical for promoting their rights and well-being within the criminal justice system. Advocacy efforts should focus on increasing funding and resources for legal representation and advocacy services, as well as promoting greater awareness and understanding of the legal rights of individuals with ID/DD.

4. **Promoting research and data collection**: Advocacy efforts should also focus on promoting research and data collection on the experiences and outcomes of individuals with ID/DD who are involved in the criminal justice system. This may involve advocating for increased funding for research and evaluation, as well as promoting greater collaboration and data-sharing among researchers, policymakers, and practitioners.

5. **Building coalitions and partnerships**: Effective advocacy and policy change often require building strong coalitions and partnerships among a range of stakeholders, including individuals with ID/DD and their families, service providers, criminal justice professionals, policymakers, and community leaders. Building these partnerships can help to promote greater awareness and understanding of the needs and challenges faced by individuals with ID/DD, as well as mobilize resources and support for advocacy and policy change efforts.

Ultimately, advocacy and policy change efforts must be grounded in a strong commitment to promoting the rights, dignity, and well-being of individuals with ID/DD who are at high risk for involvement in the criminal justice system. By working collaboratively and strategically to address the systemic barriers and

disparities faced by this population, professionals and advocates can help to

promote a more just and equitable society for all individuals, regardless of their

disability status or criminal justice involvement. This work requires ongoing

dedication, perseverance, and a willingness to challenge the status quo and

advocate for meaningful and lasting change.

Chapter VIII. Caregiver and Staff Training

A. Importance of training caregivers and staff in MOTAB principles

Training caregivers and staff in the principles and strategies of Management of Techniques and Behaviors (MOTAB) is essential for promoting the effective and consistent implementation of behavioral interventions for individuals with ID/DD who are at high risk for involvement in the criminal justice system. Caregivers and staff play a critical role in supporting individuals with ID/DD in their daily lives, and their knowledge, skills, and attitudes can have a significant impact on the success and sustainability of behavioral interventions.

There are several key reasons why training caregivers and staff in MOTAB principles is important, including:

1. Promoting consistency and continuity of care: Training caregivers and staff in MOTAB principles can help to ensure that behavioral interventions are implemented consistently and effectively across different settings and contexts. This is particularly important for individuals with ID/DD, who may have difficulty generalizing skills and behaviors from one setting to another.

2. Enhancing the effectiveness of interventions: Caregivers and staff who are trained in MOTAB principles are better equipped to recognize and respond to challenging behaviors proactively and positively, which can help to prevent escalation and promote positive outcomes. They are also better able to support individuals with ID/DD in developing new skills and behaviors, which can enhance the overall effectiveness of behavioral interventions.

3. Reducing the risk of burnout and turnover: Caring for individuals with ID/DD who are at high risk for involvement in the criminal justice system can be a challenging and emotionally demanding job. Training caregivers and staff in MOTAB principles can help to reduce the risk of burnout and turnover by providing them with the knowledge, skills, and support they need to manage challenging behaviors effectively and maintain their well-being.

4. Promoting a positive and empowering approach: MOTAB principles emphasize a positive and strengths-based approach to behavior support, which can help to promote a more empowering and respectful relationship between caregivers and individuals with ID/DD. By focusing on the individual's unique strengths, preferences, and goals, caregivers and staff can help to promote a sense of self-determination and autonomy, which can enhance the individual's overall quality of life.

Training caregivers and staff in MOTAB principles should be an ongoing process that includes both initial training and ongoing support and supervision. Initial training should provide caregivers and staff with a foundational understanding of the principles and strategies of MOTAB, as well as specific skills and techniques for managing challenging behaviors and supporting positive behavior change. Ongoing support and supervision should provide opportunities for caregivers and staff to receive feedback and guidance on their implementation of MOTAB principles, as well as to problem-solve and adapt interventions as needed.

Training should also be tailored to the specific needs and roles of different caregivers and staff, such as direct support professionals, behavioral specialists, and administrators. It should be provided in a variety of formats, such as in-person workshops, online modules, and on-the-job coaching and mentoring. Effective training should also be culturally responsive and inclusive and should take into account the diverse backgrounds and experiences of caregivers and staff.

B. Strategies for promoting consistency and generalization across settings

Promoting consistency and generalization of behavioral interventions across different settings and contexts is critical for supporting individuals with ID/DD who are at high risk for involvement in the criminal justice system. Consistency refers to the extent to which interventions are implemented in the same way across different caregivers, settings, and situations, while generalization refers to the extent to which skills and behaviors learned in one setting are transferred and applied in other settings.

There are several key strategies for promoting consistency and generalization of behavioral interventions across settings, including:

1. Developing clear and specific behavior support plans: Behavior support plans should be developed collaboratively with the individual and their support team, and should specify the target behaviors, intervention strategies, and desired outcomes. Plans should be written in clear and concise language, and should include specific instructions for implementation across different settings and situations.

2. Providing ongoing training and support for caregivers and staff: As discussed in the previous section, providing ongoing training and support for caregivers and staff is critical for promoting consistency and generalization of interventions. Training should include opportunities for practice and feedback, as well as ongoing coaching and mentoring to support the implementation of interventions in real-world settings.

3. Using positive reinforcement and feedback: Using positive reinforcement and feedback can help to promote consistency and generalization of interventions by reinforcing desired behaviors and providing motivation for continued implementation. Positive reinforcement can include praise, acknowledgment, and tangible rewards, and should be provided consistently and immediately following the desired behavior.

4. Incorporating naturalistic teaching strategies: Naturalistic teaching strategies involve embedding learning opportunities within the individual's daily routines and activities, rather than relying solely on structured training sessions. This approach can help to promote the generalization of skills and behaviors by providing opportunities for practice and reinforcement in real-world settings.

5. Collaborating with other service providers and support systems:

Collaborating with other service providers and support systems, such as schools, vocational programs, and community organizations, can help to promote consistency and generalization of interventions across different settings. This may involve sharing information about the individual's behavior support plan, providing training and support for other service providers, and coordinating interventions across different settings.

6. Monitoring and evaluating progress: Regularly monitoring and evaluating progress can help to identify areas where consistency and generalization may be lacking, and to make adjustments to interventions as needed. This may involve collecting data on the individual's behavior and progress, as well as soliciting feedback from caregivers, staff, and other service providers.

7. Promoting self-management and self-advocacy: Promoting self-management and self-advocacy skills can help individuals with ID/DD to take a more active role in their behavior support, and to generalize skills and behaviors across different settings. This may involve teaching individuals to monitor their behavior, set goals for themselves, and advocate for their own needs and preferences.

Promoting consistency and generalization of behavioral interventions requires a coordinated and collaborative approach that involves all members of the individual's support team. It also requires ongoing monitoring, evaluation, and adaptation to ensure that interventions remain effective and relevant over time. By using a range of strategies to promote consistency and generalization, professionals and caregivers can help to support individuals with ID/DD in achieving their goals and living fulfilling lives in the community.

C. Self-care and burnout prevention for caregivers and staff

Caring for individuals with ID/DD who are at high risk for involvement in the criminal justice system can be a challenging and emotionally demanding job. Caregivers and staff may experience high levels of stress, compassion fatigue, and burnout, which can negatively impact their well-being as well as the quality of care they provide. Self-care and burnout prevention strategies are therefore critical for promoting the health and well-being of caregivers and staff, and for ensuring the sustainability and effectiveness of behavioral interventions.

There are several key strategies for promoting self-care and preventing burnout among caregivers and staff, including:

1. **Encouraging regular self-care practices**: Caregivers and staff should be encouraged to engage in regular self-care practices that promote physical, emotional, and mental well-being. This may include exercise, healthy eating, sufficient sleep, stress management techniques (e.g., meditation, deep breathing), and engaging in enjoyable activities outside of work.

2. **Providing access to employee assistance programs and mental health resources**: Organizations should provide access to employee assistance programs and mental health resources, such as counseling and therapy services, to support the well-being of caregivers and staff. These resources should be easily accessible and confidential and should be promoted as a normal and valuable part of self-care.

3. **Fostering a supportive and collaborative work environment**: A supportive and collaborative work environment can help to reduce stress and burnout among caregivers and staff. This may involve regular team meetings and communication,

opportunities for peer support and mentoring, and a culture of open communication and mutual respect.

4. Providing ongoing training and professional development opportunities: Providing ongoing training and professional development opportunities can help caregivers and staff feel more competent and confident in their roles, which can reduce stress and burnout. Training should focus not only on technical skills and knowledge but also on self-care strategies and stress management techniques.

5. Encouraging work-life balance and flexible scheduling: Encouraging work-life balance and flexible scheduling can help to reduce stress and burnout by allowing caregivers and staff to attend to their own needs and responsibilities outside of work. This may involve offering flexible work hours, paid time off, and other benefits that support work-life balance.

6. Recognizing and rewarding staff for their contributions: Recognizing and rewarding staff for their contributions can help to promote job satisfaction and reduce burnout. This may involve formal recognition programs, such as employee of the month awards or bonuses, as well as informal recognition and appreciation from

supervisors and colleagues.

7. Regularly assessing and addressing workplace stressors: Regularly

assessing and addressing workplace stressors can help to identify and mitigate

sources of stress and burnout among caregivers and staff. This may involve

conducting regular surveys or focus groups to gather feedback from staff, as well

as implementing strategies to address identified stressors, such as workload

management, conflict resolution, and improving communication and collaboration.

Promoting self-care and preventing burnout among caregivers and staff requires

a comprehensive and ongoing approach that involves both individual and

organizational strategies. It also requires a culture of support and prioritization of

staff well-being, as well as regular monitoring and evaluation to ensure that

strategies are effective and relevant over time. By investing in the well-being of

caregivers and staff, organizations can promote the sustainability and

effectiveness of behavioral interventions, and ultimately improve outcomes for

individuals with ID/DD who are at high risk for involvement in the criminal justice

system.

<u>Chapter IX. Monitoring Progress and Evaluating Outcomes</u>

<u>A. Data collection and analysis methods</u>

Data collection and analysis are critical components of monitoring progress and evaluating outcomes for individuals with ID/DD who are receiving behavioral interventions through the Management of Techniques and Behaviors (MOTAB) approach. Data can provide valuable information about the effectiveness of interventions, the individual's progress toward goals, and areas where modifications or additional support may be needed.

There are several key methods for collecting and analyzing data in the context of MOTAB interventions, including:

1. Direct observation: Direct observation involves systematically observing and recording the individual's behavior in real-time, either in person or through video recording. Observers may use standardized tools, such as frequency counts or interval recording, to track the occurrence and duration of target behaviors. Direct observation can provide valuable information about the context and antecedents of behavior, as well as the individual's response to interventions.

2. Behavioral checklists and rating scales: Behavioral checklists and rating scales are standardized tools that allow caregivers and staff to rate the frequency, intensity, and severity of target behaviors over a specified period. These tools can be completed by multiple informants, such as caregivers, teachers, and therapists, to provide a more comprehensive picture of the individual's behavior across different settings and contexts.

3. Functional behavior assessments: Functional behavior assessments (FBAs) are a systematic process for identifying the antecedents, consequences, and functions of an individual's behavior. FBAs may involve a combination of direct observation, caregiver interviews, and record reviews, and can provide valuable information about the underlying reasons for behavior and potential intervention strategies.

4. Progress monitoring tools: Progress monitoring tools are standardized assessments that are administered regularly to track the individual's progress toward specific goals or outcomes. These tools may assess a range of domains, such as adaptive behavior, social skills, or mental health symptoms, and can provide valuable information about the effectiveness of interventions over time.

5. Stakeholder feedback: Stakeholder feedback, such as input from the individual, their family members, and other service providers, can provide valuable qualitative information about the individual's progress and the effectiveness of interventions. Feedback may be gathered through interviews, surveys, or focus groups, and can help to identify areas of strength and areas for improvement.

Once data has been collected, it must be analyzed and interpreted to inform decision-making and guide future interventions. Data analysis may involve a range of techniques, such as:

1. Visual analysis: Visual analysis involves graphing data over time to identify trends, patterns, and changes in behavior. This can help to identify the effectiveness of interventions, as well as potential areas for modification or additional support.

2. Statistical analysis: Statistical analysis involves using mathematical techniques to summarize and interpret data, such as calculating means, standard deviations, and effect sizes. This can help to identify significant changes in behavior over time, as well as the magnitude of intervention effects.

3. Qualitative analysis: Qualitative analysis involves systematically reviewing and interpreting non-numerical data, such as stakeholder feedback or open-ended survey responses. This can help to identify common themes or patterns in the data, as well as potential areas for improvement or further exploration.

Effective data collection and analysis requires a collaborative and systematic approach that involves all members of the individual's support team. It also requires regular monitoring and evaluation to ensure that data is being collected and analyzed reliably and validly and that interventions are being modified as needed based on the data. By using data to inform decision-making and guide interventions, professionals and caregivers can promote the effectiveness and sustainability of MOTAB interventions, and ultimately improve outcomes for individuals with ID/DD who are at high risk for involvement in the criminal justice system.

<u>**B. Assessing the effectiveness of MOTAB interventions**</u>

Assessing the effectiveness of Management of Techniques and Behaviors (MOTAB) interventions is critical for ensuring that individuals with ID/DD who are at high risk for involvement in the criminal justice system are receiving the most appropriate and effective support possible. Effectiveness can be assessed at both the individual and program level and may involve a range of indicators and outcomes.

At the individual level, assessing the effectiveness of MOTAB interventions may involve:

1. **Tracking changes in target behaviors:** Tracking changes in the frequency, intensity, and duration of target behaviors over time can provide valuable information about the effectiveness of interventions. This may involve comparing baseline data to post-intervention data or tracking progress throughout an intervention.

2. Assessing progress towards goals: Assessing the individual's progress towards specific goals or outcomes, such as increasing adaptive behavior skills or reducing criminal justice involvement, can provide valuable information about the effectiveness of interventions. This may involve using standardized assessment tools or progress monitoring measures, as well as gathering feedback from the individual and their support team.

3. Evaluating quality of life outcomes: Evaluating the individual's overall quality of life, including their social relationships, community participation, and personal well-being, can provide valuable information about the broader impact of interventions. This may involve using standardized quality-of-life measures, as well as gathering feedback from the individual and their support network.

At the program level, assessing the effectiveness of MOTAB interventions may involve:

1. Tracking program outcomes: Tracking program-level outcomes, such as the number of individuals served, the types of interventions provided, and the overall success rates, can provide valuable information about the effectiveness of the program as a whole. This may involve using program evaluation tools or conducting regular audits or reviews.

2. **Comparing outcomes to benchmarks**: Comparing program outcomes to established benchmarks or standards, such as national or state averages for similar programs, can provide valuable information about the relative effectiveness of the program. This may involve participating in external evaluations or accreditation processes, as well as conducting internal benchmarking analyses.

3. **Gathering stakeholder feedback**: Gathering feedback from a range of stakeholders, including individuals served, family members, staff, and community partners, can provide valuable information about the perceived effectiveness and impact of the program. This may involve conducting surveys, focus groups, or interviews, as well as analyzing complaint and grievance data.

Assessing the effectiveness of MOTAB interventions requires a comprehensive and ongoing approach that involves multiple methods and perspectives. It also requires a commitment to continuous quality improvement, and a willingness to modify interventions and supports based on the data and feedback received. By regularly assessing the effectiveness of interventions and making data-driven decisions, professionals and caregivers can ensure that individuals with ID/DD who are at high risk for involvement in the criminal justice system are receiving the most appropriate and effective support possible.

C. Modifying support plans based on individual progress and changing needs

Modifying support plans based on individual progress and changing needs is a critical component of providing effective and person-centered support to individuals with ID/DD who are at high risk for involvement in the criminal justice system. Support plans should be viewed as living documents that are regularly reviewed and updated based on the individual's progress, challenges, and evolving needs and preferences.

There are several key considerations for modifying support plans based on individual progress and changing needs, including:

1. **Reviewing data and progress monitoring information**: Regularly reviewing data and progress monitoring information can provide valuable insights into the

individual's progress towards goals, as well as areas where additional support or modification may be needed. This may involve analyzing trends in behavioral data, reviewing progress towards objectives, and gathering feedback from the individual and their support team.

2. **Assessing changes in the individual's needs and preferences:** Assessing changes in the individual's needs and preferences over time can help to ensure that support plans remain relevant and person-centered. This may involve conducting regular assessments or interviews with the individual and their support network, as well as observing changes in behavior or functioning that may indicate a need for additional support or modification.

3. **Collaborating with the individual and their support team:** Collaborating with the individual and their support team is critical for ensuring that modifications to support plans are appropriate, feasible, and aligned with the individual's goals and preferences. This may involve holding regular team meetings or case conferences, as well as seeking input and feedback from the individual and their support network throughout the modification process.

4. Considering the use of new or different interventions: Considering the use of new or different interventions may be necessary when the individual's progress has plateaued or when challenging behaviors persist despite the use of current interventions. This may involve conducting a functional behavior assessment to identify the underlying functions of behavior, as well as exploring new or alternative intervention strategies that may be more effective for the individual.

5. Addressing changes in the individual's environment or circumstances: Addressing changes in the individual's environment or circumstances, such as a change in living situation or a significant life event, may require modifications to support plans to ensure that interventions remain relevant and effective. This may involve conducting a new assessment of the individual's needs and preferences, as well as collaborating with other service providers or support systems to ensure continuity of care.

6. Documenting and communicating changes: Documenting and communicating changes to support plans is critical for ensuring that all members of the individual's support team are aware of and able to implement the modifications. This may involve updating written support plans, as well as providing training and support to staff and caregivers to ensure that modifications are implemented consistently and effectively.

Modifying support plans based on individual progress and changing needs requires a flexible and responsive approach that prioritizes the individual's well-being and autonomy. It also requires ongoing collaboration and communication among all members of the individual's support team, as well as a commitment to using data and feedback to inform decision-making and guide interventions. By regularly reviewing and modifying support plans based on individual needs and progress, professionals and caregivers can promote the effectiveness and sustainability of MOTAB interventions, and ultimately improve outcomes for individuals with ID/DD who are at high risk for involvement in the criminal justice system.

Chapter X. Case Studies and "Real-world" Applications

Fictitious Examples

A. Examples of successful MOTAB implementation

The Management of Techniques and Behaviors (MOTAB) approach has been successfully implemented in a variety of settings and contexts to support individuals with ID/DD who are at high risk for involvement in the criminal justice system. The following case studies provide fictitious examples of successful MOTAB implementation and highlight this approach's potential benefits and outcomes.

1. Case Study 1: John

John is a 32-year-old man with mild ID and a history of aggression and property destruction. He had been arrested several times for assault and had spent time in jail. After his most recent arrest, John was referred to a community-based program that used the MOTAB approach to support individuals with ID/DD who were at risk for criminal justice involvement.

The program began by conducting a comprehensive assessment of John's needs, strengths, and risk factors. This included a functional behavior assessment to identify the underlying functions of his aggressive behavior, as well as an assessment of his adaptive behavior skills and mental health needs. Based on this assessment, the program developed an individualized support plan for John that included:

- Positive behavior support strategies to prevent and reduce aggressive behavior, such as providing choices and using visual schedules

- Skill-building interventions to teach John alternative coping strategies and communication skills

- Mental health treatment to address underlying anxiety and trauma

- Vocational training and supported employment to help John develop job skills and find meaningful work

The program also provided training and support to John's family members and caregivers to ensure that interventions were implemented consistently across settings. John participated in the program for 18 months and made significant progress toward his goals. He learned new coping strategies and communication skills, obtained a part-time job, and had no further arrests or incidents of aggression.

2. Case Study 2: Sarah

Sarah is a 24-year-old woman with moderate ID and a history of self-injurious behavior and sexual offending. She had been arrested for public indecency and was at risk for further legal involvement. Sarah was referred to a specialized treatment program that used the MOTAB approach to support individuals with ID/DD who had engaged in sexual offending.

The program conducted a comprehensive assessment of Sarah's needs and risk factors, including a sexual behavior risk assessment and a functional behavior assessment of her self-injurious behavior. Based on this assessment, the program developed an individualized support plan for Sarah that included:

- Positive behavior support strategies to prevent and reduce self-injurious behavior, such as providing sensory interventions and using a token economy system

- Cognitive-behavioral therapy to address distorted thinking patterns and improve decision-making skills

- Sex education and social skills training to improve Sarah's understanding of healthy relationships and boundaries

- Family therapy to improve communication and support within Sarah's family system

The program also collaborated with Sarah's probation officer and other community providers to ensure a coordinated and comprehensive approach to her care. Sarah participated in the program for 24 months and made significant progress toward her goals. She learned new coping strategies and social skills, developed a better understanding of healthy relationships, and had no further incidents of sexual offending or self-injurious behavior.

These case studies demonstrate the potential effectiveness of the MOTAB approach in supporting individuals with ID/DD who are at high risk for involvement in the criminal justice system. **By conducting comprehensive assessments, developing individualized support plans, and providing training and support to caregivers and staff, programs using the MOTAB approach can help individuals develop new skills, reduce challenging behaviors, and avoid further legal involvement.** Successful implementation of the MOTAB approach requires collaboration, communication, and a commitment to using evidence-based practices to support individuals with ID/DD in achieving their goals and living fulfilling lives in the community.

<u>**B. Lessons learned and recommendations for overcoming challenges**</u>

Implementing the Management of Techniques and Behaviors (MOTAB) approach to support individuals with ID/DD who are at high risk for involvement in the criminal justice system can present a range of challenges and obstacles. However, by learning from the experiences of successful programs and practitioners, it is possible to identify key lessons and recommendations for overcoming these challenges and promoting effective implementation of the MOTAB approach.

Some of the key lessons learned and recommendations for overcoming challenges in implementing the MOTAB approach include:

1. **Conduct comprehensive assessments:** Conducting comprehensive assessments of individuals' needs, strengths, and risk factors is critical for developing effective and individualized support plans. Assessments should include a range of methods and tools, such as functional behavior assessments, adaptive behavior assessments, and risk assessments, and should involve input from multiple

stakeholders, including the individual, their family members, and other service providers.

2. **Develop collaborative partnerships:** Developing collaborative partnerships with a range of stakeholders, including criminal justice agencies, mental health providers, and community organizations, is essential for providing coordinated and comprehensive support to individuals with ID/DD who are at high risk for involvement in the criminal justice system. Partnerships should be based on clear communication, shared goals, and a commitment to using evidence-based practices to support individuals in achieving their goals.

3. **Provide ongoing training and support:** Providing ongoing training and support to caregivers, staff, and other service providers is critical for ensuring the consistent and effective implementation of the MOTAB approach. Training should cover a range of topics, including positive behavior support strategies, crisis intervention techniques, and cultural competence, and should be provided in a variety of formats, such as in-person workshops, online modules, and on-the-job coaching.

4. Use data to inform decision-making: Using data to inform decision-making and guide interventions is essential for promoting the effectiveness and sustainability of the MOTAB approach. Data should be collected and analyzed regularly, using a range of methods and tools, such as direct observation, behavioral checklists, and progress monitoring measures. Data should be used to identify areas of strength and areas for improvement and to make modifications to interventions as needed based on individual progress and changing needs.

5. Promote self-determination and person-centered planning: Promoting self-determination and person-centered planning is critical for ensuring that interventions are aligned with individuals' goals, preferences, and values. Individuals with ID/DD should be actively involved in the planning and implementation of their support plans, and should be provided with opportunities to make choices and direct their care to the greatest extent possible.

6. Address systemic barriers and challenges: Addressing systemic barriers and challenges, such as limited funding, lack of community resources, and stigma and discrimination, is essential for promoting the sustainability and effectiveness of the MOTAB approach. This may involve advocating for policy and funding changes, developing new partnerships and collaborations, and promoting public awareness and education about the needs and strengths of individuals with ID/DD who are at high risk for involvement in the criminal justice system.

7. Promote cultural competence and responsiveness: Promoting cultural competence and responsiveness is critical for ensuring that interventions are appropriate and effective for individuals from diverse cultural and linguistic backgrounds. This may involve providing training and support to staff and caregivers on cultural competence, involving family members and community leaders in the planning and implementation of interventions, and adapting interventions to be culturally relevant and responsive.

By incorporating these lessons and recommendations into the planning and implementation of the MOTAB approach, programs and practitioners can overcome challenges and promote the effective and sustainable support of individuals with ID/DD who are at high risk for involvement in the criminal justice system. Successful implementation of the MOTAB approach requires ongoing learning, adaptation, and collaboration, as well as a commitment to using evidence-based practices and person-centered approaches to support individuals in achieving their

goals and living fulfilling lives in the community.

<u>**Chapter XI. Resources and References**</u>

<u>**A. Recommended reading and additional resources**</u>

There are a variety of recommended readings and additional resources available for individuals and organizations interested in learning more about the Management of Techniques and Behaviors (MOTAB) approach and supporting individuals with ID/DD who are at high risk for involvement in the criminal justice system. Some of these resources include:

- The Arc's National Center on Criminal Justice and Disability

- The National Association for the Dually Diagnosed (NADD)

- The American Association on Intellectual and Developmental Disabilities

- The National Center on Disability and Abuse

- The National Council on Crime and Delinquency

Policy and advocacy organizations:

- The Bazelon Center for Mental Health Law

- The National Disability Rights Network

- The National Alliance on Mental Illness (NAMI)

- The American Civil Liberties Union (ACLU)

These resources can provide valuable information and guidance on best practices, evidence-based interventions, and policy and advocacy efforts related to supporting individuals with ID/DD who are at high risk for involvement in the criminal justice system. They can also serve as a starting point for connecting with other professionals and organizations working in this field, and for staying up-to-date on the latest research and developments.

B. Professional organizations and training opportunities

There are several professional organizations and training opportunities available for individuals and organizations interested in learning more about the MOTAB approach and supporting individuals with ID/DD who are at high risk for involvement in the criminal justice system. Some of these include:

1. Professional organizations:

- The National Association for the Dually Diagnosed (NADD): NADD is an interdisciplinary membership organization that provides education, training, and support for professionals working with individuals who have both ID/DD and mental health needs. NADD offers a variety of resources, including conferences, webinars, and publications, as well as an accreditation and certification program for programs serving this population.

- The American Association on Intellectual and Developmental Disabilities (AAIDD): AAIDD is a professional organization that promotes progressive policies, sound research, effective practices, and universal human rights for people with intellectual and developmental disabilities. AAIDD offers a variety of resources, including conferences, webinars, and publications, as well as a certification program for professionals working in this field.

- The Association for Positive Behavior Support (APBS): APBS is an international organization dedicated to promoting research-based strategies that combine applied behavior analysis and biomedical science with person-centered values and systems change to increase quality of life and decrease problem behaviors. APBS offers a variety of resources, including conferences, webinars, and publications, as well as a certification program for professionals working in this field.

2. Training opportunities:

- The NADD Annual Conference: The NADD Annual Conference is a premier event for professionals working with individuals who have both ID/DD and mental health needs. The conference features a variety of keynote speakers, workshops, and networking opportunities, and covers topics such as assessment, intervention, and policy and advocacy.

- The AAIDD Annual Conference: The AAIDD Annual Conference is a premier event for professionals working in the field of intellectual and developmental disabilities. The conference features a variety of keynote speakers, workshops, and networking opportunities, and covers topics such as research, practice, and policy.

- The APBS International Conference: The APBS International Conference is a premier event for professionals working in the field of positive behavior support. The conference features a variety of keynote speakers, workshops, and networking opportunities, and covers topics such as assessment, intervention, and systems change.

- Online training modules and webinars: Many professional organizations and training providers offer online training modules and webinars on topics related to supporting individuals with ID/DD who are at high risk for involvement in the criminal justice system. These can be a convenient and cost-effective way to access training and professional development opportunities.

Participating in professional organizations and training opportunities can help individuals and organizations stay up-to-date on best practices, evidence-based interventions, and policy and advocacy efforts related to supporting individuals with ID/DD who are at high risk for involvement in the criminal justice system. They can also provide valuable networking and collaboration opportunities and can help to build a sense of community and shared purpose among professionals working in this field.

<u>**C. References cited throughout the guidebook**</u>

The following is a list of references cited throughout the MOTAB guidebook:

1. American Association on Intellectual and Developmental Disabilities. (2021). Definition of intellectual disability.

2. Association for Positive Behavior Support. (2021). What is positive behavior support?

3. Bazelon Center for Mental Health Law. (2021). Criminal justice.

4. Fletcher, R. J., & Rowe, D. M. (2017). The NADD accreditation and certification program: Standards and procedures manual for programs serving individuals with intellectual and developmental disabilities and mental health needs. NADD Press.

5. Lindsay, W. R., & Taylor, J. L. (Eds.). (2018). Effective intervention for offenders with intellectual disabilities. Routledge.

6. Lindsay, W. R., Craig, L. A., & Griffiths, D. (Eds.). (2019). The handbook of forensic intellectual disability. Wiley-Blackwell.

7. National Association of State Directors of Developmental Disabilities Services & National Association of State Mental Health Program Directors. (2015). Intellectual disability and the criminal justice system: Solutions through collaboration.

8. National Center on Disability and Abuse. (2021). About us.

9. National Council on Crime and Delinquency. (2021). Intellectual and developmental disabilities.

10. The Arc's National Center on Criminal Justice and Disability. (2021). About.

These references provide a wealth of information and guidance on best practices, evidence-based interventions, and policy and advocacy efforts related to supporting individuals with ID/DD who are at high risk for involvement in the criminal justice system. They can serve as a valuable resource for individuals and organizations looking to deepen their understanding of this complex and challenging field and to identify strategies and approaches that can be adapted and applied in their work.

XII. Appendices

A. Assessment tools and templates

The following assessment tools and templates can be used to support the implementation of the Management of Techniques and Behaviors (MOTAB) approach:

1. Functional Behavior Assessment (FBA) template: This template provides a structured format for conducting an FBA, including identifying the target behavior, gathering information about the antecedents and consequences of the behavior, and developing hypotheses about the function of the behavior.

2. Behavioral Support Plan (BSP) template: This template provides a structured format for developing a BSP based on the results of an FBA, including identifying replacement behaviors, selecting intervention strategies, and developing a plan for monitoring and evaluating progress.

3. Adaptive Behavior Assessment System (ABAS-3): The ABAS-3 is a standardized assessment tool that measures adaptive behavior skills in individuals from birth to 89. It can be used to identify strengths and areas for improvement in adaptive behavior and to develop targeted interventions and supports.

4. Vineland Adaptive Behavior Scales (Vineland-3): The Vineland-3 is a standardized assessment tool that measures adaptive behavior skills in individuals from birth to 90. It can be used to identify strengths and areas for improvement in adaptive behavior and to develop targeted interventions and supports.

5. Risk-Need-Responsivity (RNR) assessment tools: RNR assessment tools, such as the Level of Service Inventory-Revised (LSI-R) and the Ohio Risk Assessment System (ORAS), can be used to assess an individual's risk for recidivism and to identify criminogenic needs that should be targeted in intervention and support plans.

6. Person-Centered Planning (PCP) templates: PCP templates, such as the Essential Lifestyle Planning (ELP) and the Personal Futures Planning (PFP) templates, can be used to facilitate a person-centered approach to intervention and support planning, by identifying the individual's strengths, preferences, and goals, and developing a plan to achieve those goals.

These assessment tools and templates can be adapted and customized to fit the specific needs and contexts of different programs and individuals. They should be used in conjunction with other sources of information, such as interviews, observations, and record reviews, to develop a comprehensive understanding of the individual's needs, strengths, and risk factors.

B. Visual support examples and resources

The following visual support examples and resources can be used to support the implementation of the MOTAB approach:

1. Visual schedules: Visual schedules use pictures, symbols, or words to represent the activities or routines that an individual needs to complete throughout the day. They can help to provide structure and predictability, reduce anxiety, and promote independence.

2. Social stories: Social stories are short, simple stories that describe a particular social situation or skill, using a combination of text and pictures. They can help individuals understand and navigate social expectations and norms and can be used to teach specific social skills or behaviors.

3. Communication boards and devices: Communication boards and devices use pictures, symbols, or voice output to allow individuals to express their needs, wants, or thoughts. They can range from low-tech options, such as picture exchange systems, to high-tech options, such as speech-generating devices.

4. Token economy systems: Token economy systems use tangible rewards, such as stickers or points, to reinforce desired behaviors. Individuals earn tokens for engaging in specific behaviors and can exchange them for preferred items or activities.

5. Visual cues and prompts: Visual cues and prompts use pictures, symbols, or gestures to remind individuals to engage in specific behaviors or to complete specific tasks. They can be used to promote independence and reduce the need for verbal prompts or reminders.

6. Video modeling: Video modeling involves creating short videos that demonstrate specific skills or behaviors, which individuals can watch and imitate. Video modeling can be particularly effective for teaching social skills, vocational skills, and daily living skills.

7. Visual boundaries and safety supports: Visual boundaries and safety supports use visual cues, such as colored tape or signs, to mark off safe or appropriate areas or to provide reminders about safety rules and expectations. They can be used to promote safety and reduce the risk of dangerous or inappropriate behaviors.

These visual support examples and resources can be adapted and customized to fit the specific needs and preferences of different individuals and contexts. They should be used in conjunction with other intervention strategies, such as positive behavior support and skill-building interventions, to promote positive behavior change and improve quality of life outcomes.

<u>C. Glossary of key terms and acronyms</u>

The following glossary provides definitions and explanations for some of the key terms and acronyms used throughout the MOTAB guidebook:

- **Adaptive behavior:** The skills and abilities that individuals need to function independently in daily life, including communication, social skills, self-care, and community living skills.

- **Antecedent:** The events or circumstances that occur immediately before a behavior, and may serve as triggers or cues for the behavior.

- **Behavior support plan (BSP):** A written document that outlines the strategies and interventions that will be used to promote positive behavior change and improve quality of life outcomes for an individual.

- **Consequence:** The events or outcomes that occur immediately after a behavior, and may serve to reinforce or discourage the behavior in the future.

- **Criminogenic needs**: The dynamic risk factors that are associated with an increased likelihood of criminal behavior, such as substance abuse, antisocial attitudes, and poor problem-solving skills.

- **Functional behavior assessment (FBA)**: A systematic process for identifying the antecedents, consequences, and functions of a particular behavior, to develop effective intervention strategies.

- **Intellectual and developmental disabilities (ID/DD)**: A group of disorders that are characterized by significant limitations in both intellectual functioning and adaptive behavior, with onset during the developmental period.

- **Positive behavior support (PBS)**: A proactive approach to behavior intervention that focuses on preventing problem behaviors, teaching replacement behaviors, and improving quality of life outcomes.

- **Recidivism**: The tendency for individuals who have been convicted of a crime to re-offend and be rearrested, reconvicted, or returned to prison.

- **Replacement behavior**: A socially appropriate behavior that serves the same function as a problem behavior, and can be taught and reinforced as an alternative to the problem behavior.

- **Risk-Need-Responsivity (RNR) model**: A framework for assessing and treating individuals who are at risk for criminal behavior, based on their level of risk, criminogenic needs, and responsivity to different intervention strategies.

- **Self-determination**: The ability to make choices and direct one's own life, based on one's preferences, values, and goals.

- **Skill-building intervention**: An intervention that focuses on teaching and reinforcing specific skills or behaviors that can help individuals to function more independently and effectively in daily life.

- **Visual support**: A type of intervention that uses pictures, symbols, or other visual cues to promote understanding, communication, and positive behavior change.

These key terms and acronyms are used throughout the MOTAB guidebook to describe the principles, strategies, and tools that can be used to support individuals with ID/DD who are at high risk for involvement in the criminal justice system. Understanding these terms and concepts can help practitioners and caregivers communicate more effectively, identify appropriate interventions and supports, and promote positive outcomes for the individuals they serve.

www.ingramcontent.com/pod-product-compliance
Lightning Source LLC
Chambersburg PA
CBHW072247260726
48659CB00004BA/1436